THE

WESTERN MARYLAND RAILROAD

AND

His Honor the Mayor of Baltimore,

VERSUS

THE BALT. & OHIO RAILROAD.

BALTIMORE.

1863.

THE WESTERN MARYLAND AND BALTIMORE AND OHIO RAIL ROADS.

The Western Maryland Railroad is a branch of the Northern Central Railroad, commencing at the Relay House on the latter road, eight miles from Baltimore, and running thence about forty miles to "Union Bridge," in the valley of Little Pipe Creek. It was opened so far not long since, and efforts are now being made to extend it to Hagarstown. An appeal to the capitalists of this city for the means required for this extension was lately made by a writer over the signature of "Carroll County," and his Honor the Mayor of Baltimore has presented the claims of the road in very earnest and emphatic terms in his recent message to the Councils, wherein he says, "the one great object of the President and Directors of this road is its speedy completion to Hagarstown, and I am happy to say the directors are a unit on this point." In his previous notice of the Baltimore and Ohio Railroad, and the destruction, a second time, of a part of it by the rebels, he advises the "adoption of the Washington County route, which, (he says,) it was well known was the original design," and adds that "the citizens of our State were grievously wronged by this diversion." His Honor proceeds to say, that "when the Western Maryland road is completed to Hagarstown, it will be but ten miles to Fort Frederick, the point where the Baltimore and Ohio Railroad returns to Maryland after its digression into Virginia," and further, that "if the two roads were there connected, a shorter route by *forty-five* miles to Baltimore would be furnished than that now in use by the Baltimore and Ohio Company,"—and again, "if the Western Maryland Railroad was completed to Hagarstown, and the ten miles of road built to Fort Frederick, it would be a much more reasonable undertaking than to expend a large amount of money in the re-construction of the Baltimore and Ohio Railroad, which may possibly be destroyed again."

The Chief Magistrate of the City thus appears as the champion of a new route to the West, to supersede the Baltimore and Ohio Railroad, or at least that part which lies within the State of Virginia. Now it must be remarked in the first place, that his Honor has been led to make some extraordinary mistakes as to the extent of our great western road, which lies within Virginia territory. He says that it returns to Maryland at Fort Frederick, whereas in fact, it does not return to Maryland until within six miles east of Cumberland, some sixty-two miles *beyond* Fort Frederick! The Mayor would thus make it out that but thirty miles of the Baltimore and Ohio Railroad is in Virginia, while in fact, ninety-two miles is on the soil of that State, east of Cumberland. Again he makes the distance from Baltimore to Hagarstown, by the Western Maryland Railroad but *eighty* miles, whereas it is *eighty-eight* miles by the preferred and undoubtedly preferable route via Emmittsburgh. Further, he calls the distance from Hagarstown to Fort Frederick *ten* miles, whereas it is *twenty* miles by the nearest feasible route. If we put these distances together we will see that the distance from Baltimore to Fort Frederick by the Western Maryland route, would be 108 miles, while to the same point by the Baltimore and Ohio Railroad it is in fact but 112 miles, showing a saving of but *four* miles by the Western Maryland instead of *forty-five* miles, as asserted by his Honor the Mayor—and even this small saving is effected at the expense of crossing a mountain 1,000 feet high, which the Baltimore and Ohio Railroad altogether avoids.

It is thus shown that the assumptions of the Mayor in regard to the *facts* of the case being wholly unfounded, his reasoning based thereon must fall to the ground. But how, it may be asked, came his Honor to be so fearfully misinformed as to these facts. How came he to know so little of the location of the great artery of the interior trade of the city of which he is Chief Magistrate—what apology can be made for the exhibition of such ignorance upon a subject upon which he should have been so thoroughly informed, and especially when he undertakes to write authoritatively about the internal improvements of the city in whose legislative councils and executive chair he has sat so long. The problem is a puzzling one indeed, but it is of easier solution than might be supposed. The Mayor has obtained all his facts and conclusions too, from sources interested in deceiving him, and by whom his enthusiasm for the Western Maryland Railroad has been turned to good account to subserve their selfish purposes.

We know that "it is good to be zealously affected in a good thing"—but it endangers the loss of our balance to pursue even a good thing with so much eagerness as to stumble over the obstacles in the way, which we overlook in our haste to grasp the object at which we are aiming. We may put this charitable construction upon his Honor's course in this matter, and place the responsibility for the gross mistakes he has made upon those who have been guilty from interested motives, of misleading him, upon a subject of such vital importance to our city.

But let us see if the Mayor and his advisers, in asserting that what they call the "Washington County route," *was* the "original design,"—and that "the citizens of our State were grievously wronged in its diversion," are any nearer being right than they are in regard to the relative lengths and point of junction of the routes. It will be necessary to go briefly into the early history of the Baltimore and Ohio Railroad to shed the proper light on this point. In the year 1827, that Company having organized itself and obtained from the United States Government the aid of several members of its corps of topographical engineers, proceeded to examine thoroughly the whole country between this city and the Potomac river at Williamsport, in Washington County. These engineers, whose competency for the duty cannot be questioned, made instrumental surveys of all the practicable routes between those points. The country between Baltimore and the first range of mountains called the "South Mountain," was distinguished by one prominent feature, a ridge of land about thirty miles from Baltimore in a direct line, ranging from 700 to 800 feet above tide, running nearly N. E. and S. W., and dividing the waters of the Patapsco from those of the Monocacy. This ridge presented here and there depressions at the heads of streams rising near its summit and flowing in opposite directions into those two rivers. Lines were run across it at several of those low places, these lines following up the streams on the Patapsco side, and then following down those on the Monocacy side. Passes were found at not less than five of those depressions, through any one of which the road might be successfully carried over to the Monocacy valley. That valley however being reached, the great mountain range bounding it on the west, presented a barrier of twice the elevation of the previous ridge. How best to pass this mountain was then the most important question to be decided, and the Company's engineers without hesitation, preferred to go *round* the mountain at the "Point of Rocks," than to go *over* it at "Harman's Gap." Any one who chooses to refer to the Third Annual Report of the Company in 1829, page 6, will see a comparison of the different routes in the appended note, which reads thus:

"By reference to the maps and profiles which accompany this report, the advantages of the route selected, and its decided preference over all others that have been examined, will at once become manifest. The *equated* distance, (that is where the elevations to be passed over are expressed by their equivalents in miles) from Baltimore to Williamsport, along the route adopted, is $129\frac{79}{100}$ miles, whilst the distance in equated miles by the most favorable route north of it is $162\frac{90}{100}$ miles. It should be observed that no route was discovered north of the Point of Rocks with less than four summits, while the route selected has necessarily but one summit requiring stationary or local power."

This one summit (at Mount Airy Station on the Baltimore and Ohio Railroad) which was at first passed by horse power, has for twenty-five years been crossed by locomotives.

The distance from Baltimore to Williamsport, by the Point of Rocks on the line surveyed in 1828, was 104.60

miles by the surveys just mentioned, and the heights overcome, 886 feet, while the shortest route by Harman's Gap over the South Mountain was $95\frac{43}{100}$ miles, and heights overcome, 2,375 feet, showing a difference of $9\frac{1}{6}$ miles in distance *against* the Point of Rocks, and 1,489 feet in height overcome *in its favor.* Now this route by Harman's Gap was nearly identical with that of the Western Maryland Railroad via Westminster, as far as the latter has been built to Union Bridge, beyond which point the Western Maryland Railroad diverges northward to Emmittsburg, not only to accommodate that flourishing town, but to obtain an easier ascent of the mountain at whose foot it stands. The Harman's Gap route of the old surveys, went by Mechanicstown, apparently a more direct course, but as the distance to Williamsport, six miles beyond Hagarstown, is about the same on both lines, it seems that the Emmittsburg route, superior in all other respects, is equally short and should therefore be preferred. In fact, the mountain having to be crossed with a certain grade, (say 80 or 90 feet in a mile,) a length of line sufficient to surmount it with that grade must be obtained, and so for equal heights to be overcome, the distances must be the same. The reason why no route between the Point of Rocks and Harman's Gap was found, is that the mountain there divides into two separate ranges, between which lies the Middletown valley, so that any intermediate route would have required the crossing of *two* mountains and a deep rugged valley between them.

From these facts, developed and set forth in the Company's report, published thirty-five years ago, it must be manifest that the route of the road was decided upon proper principles, scientific and practical, and that in doing so the "grievous wrong to the citizens of our State," of which his Honor the Mayor complains, was not at all committed—but that on the contrary such a wrong would have been done to those of our citizens who nobly risked their fortunes and estates in this pioneer enterprise in the Railroad field, had any other route been taken, and a mountain 1,000 feet high crossed with high grades and abrupt curvatures, when, by going a few miles round it might be passed in the level gap of the river Potomac.

There was, it is believed, an insinuation uttered at the time and now revived, that the road was taken by *Ellicott's Mills* to please the Quaker party—but that was a minor question and had nothing to do with the route in and beyond the valley of the Monocacy. Besides, there were more Quakers on "Pipe Creek" and the Western Maryland route, than at Ellicott's Mills. The Company, moreover, must have had the very best reasons for taking the Point of Rocks route, or they would not have encountered thereat the opposition of the Chesapeake and Ohio Canal, which, by its attendant litigation, lost them much time and cost them much money. Having at length forced their way from the Point of Rocks up to Harper's Ferry, along side of the canal, they found it best to cross there at once into Virginia and keep on the Virginia side the $\frac{15}{16}$ of the whole distance to Cumberland, rather than attempt a side by side construction any farther, and so the Baltimore and Ohio Railroad has come to occupy so much Virginia soil, although his Honor the Mayor (marvellous to repeat!) was not aware of it. By this crossing at Harper's Ferry, a better connection with the rich valley of Virginia was established and several miles of distance was saved as well as heavy cost, and hence at Fort Frederick, thirty miles west of the Ferry, the Baltimore and Ohio Railroad shows a distance to Baltimore but four miles (not forty-five) greater than that of the Western Maryland Railroad, and with about 1,000 feet less height to overcome.

After having his figures thus corrected, his Honor will perhaps be less tenacious of his opinion that the Baltimore and Ohio Railroad should be abandoned and the Western Maryland should take its place to Fort Frederick, and the rather as he has by this time been informed that his favorite route would have to cross to the dangerous soil of Virginia at that point, and continue on it for no less than sixty-two miles before it re-entered the territory of our State. The Mayor however, seems, by the way, to forget that in assuming as he does, the future repeated destruction of the Baltimore and Ohio Railroad in Virginia, he is conceding the indefinite continuance of the present civil war, if not the ultimate division of the Union, and the attachment of the part of the road in that State to a Southern Confederacy.

His Honor must not forget too, that the Baltimore and Ohio Railroad after re-crossing into Maryland six miles east of Cumberland, returns into Virginia twenty-one miles west of that place, and after continuing on Virginia soil for some nine miles, and then occupying Maryland ground for thirty-one miles, finally returns to Virginia and leaves that State not again until it reaches its two termini at Wheeling and Parkersburg—each about 140 miles from the point of re-entrance. In short, out of the 486 miles of the main stem of the road, only 141 are on Maryland and 345 on Virginia soil. It is well then that the people of Baltimore should understand these plain *facts*, that they may know how much of their great western road they may have to give up if the policy recommended by their present Chief Magistrate be adopted.

True, most of the Virginia part of the road is in "West Virginia," the intended new State—but if the South should by any chance achieve her independence at all—and her solemn declarations are to be believed—she will not give up an acre of the soil of that State which has been her great battle ground, and has suffered most in her cause. That any final separation will take place is not, however, to be admitted, and hence the danger of the Virginia part of the Baltimore and Ohio Railroad must be regarded as but transient, and new routes to avoid it as wholly unnecessary. But to make the Mayor's scheme of an *entire Maryland route* complete, it would be requisite to construct a road on the Maryland side of the Potomac from Hagarstown all the way to Cumberland, and not simply to Fort Frederick, as his Honor has been deluded into believing. Now let us see what that part of his project would cost. There are satisfactory data to compute this in the numerous surveys of the Baltimore and Ohio Railroad Company made in 1836 and 1837, reported upon in the report of their engineers of February, 1838. From this report we find that the only feasible route from Fort Frederick to Cumberland, would follow the Potomac river immediately on the river margin of the Chesapeake and Ohio Canal for about twenty-eight miles—then leave it for about eighteen miles and, returning to it, follow it thence to Cumberland. Any route departing from the river to a greater extent than this would, as was well settled by the Company's extensive surveys, be inadmissible on account of the numerous mountain ranges which cross the country, and which the Potomac alone cuts through. The single practicable divergence embraced in the route described, encounters a summit 400 feet in height, and would not be advisable but for the greater difficulties attendant upon the occupation by the canal of the part of the river valley thus avoided.

Another route has indeed been spoken of, and is understood to be rather a favorite one with some of the Mayor's advisers on this subject. This route would pursue the Franklin Railroad to a point some sixteen miles from Hagerstown towards Chambersburgh. At this point it would diverge westwardly and follow the route surveyed for a railroad from Chambersburgh to Pittsburgh by the Pennsylvania state engineers in 1838. This route has been known more recently as the "Chambersburgh and Allegheny" Railroad. From the printed report of the engineer, Mr. Hagè, published January, 1839, we are informed of all the particulars of the route, which pursues a circuitous course, rendered necessary by the several mountain ranges it is compelled to pass, and passing through the town of Bedford, finally reaches the line of the Pittsburgh and Connellsville Railroad, (by a branch of some ten miles from Hagè's line,) at a point about fourteen miles west, or rather north of Cumberland. The length of the route would be 122 miles, and it would encounter ascents and descents amounting altogether to 3,859 feet, while a route following the Potomac valley on the Maryland side, with the slight divergence above described, would be ninety-seven miles between the same points, with a rise and fall of but 2,128 feet—showing a difference in its favor of twenty-five miles of distance, and 1,731 feet of rise and fall—equivalent by the common modes of computation to some thirty-three miles more. The cost of constructing a railroad upon the Maryland route through Cumberland would be something over $4,000,000, while upon the Pennsylvania route through Bedford, it would (at the same scale of prices) be $5,000,000.

It is believed that there is still a subsisting charter for the Bedford road, but that it is under the control of the Pennsylvania Central Company, who also control the Cumberland Valley and Franklin road, from Harrisburgh to Hagarstown, of which this Bedford road would be properly an extension. If Virginia then is to be avoided, and Cumberland or the Connellsville road reached by a line north of the Potomac, there can be little difficulty in deciding between the two routes described; the Bedford route having undoubtedly the solitary advantage of being out of reach of the longest range rifled cannon from the heights on the Virginia side of that river—an advantage dearly purchased however, by its other objectionable features.

It may be observed here, in this connection, that a route immediately on the Maryland shore of the Potomac would be exposed to attack and interruption almost as much as if it were on the Virginia side of the river, and hence that little increase of safety would be gained by placing the water course of but a couple of hundred yards wide between the road and its assailants.

It has been considered advisable that the citizens of Baltimore should, at this juncture, be correctly informed as to the facts of this case, and hence the preceding brief history of them has been given in order that they may not be misled as their Chief Magistrate has been by the misrepresentations of the interested parties who have obtained so unaccountable a control over his Honor's better judgment in this matter.

The city having been induced to assist in the construction of the Western Maryland Railroad as far as its present terminus, to Union Bridge, has done quite enough for that improvement. Its extension, some 12 or 13 miles farther to

Emmittsburgh at the foot of the South Mountain, and some 60 miles from Baltimore and close to the Pennsylvania line, is probably an advisable measure, and will help to make it a good local road through a fertile and populous part of our state. The city should not however, be called upon to furnish the means for this extension, as she is sufficiently involved already by her endorsement on the Company's bonds, on which although, as the Mayor says, the interest may have been heretofore punctually paid (out of the borrowed *construction* fund ?) It remains to be seen whether it and the interest on the rest of the Company's obligations will be as punctually met hereafter out of the "net earnings" of the road, which has but recently been received from the contractors in a very imperfectly finished state. It may rather be apprehended that all the net revenue to be realized for some time to come, will be required for "construction account," and the extension of the road to Emmittsburgh.

This extension as just remarked, may be a judicious operation, but let it be understood that the final termination is to be at that beautiful Maryland town, just within the borders of our state, and let the chimerical scheme of climbing a mountain a thousand feet high in order to reach Hagarstown by a circuitous, rugged and costly route, barren of trade and travel, be given up. Hagarstown should indeed, it is admitted, be brought into connection with Baltimore by rail and its trade restored in that way to our city. This, however, can be better done by a short, cheap and almost level route of some eighteen miles through Williamsport to the Baltimore and Ohio Railroad, at a point four or five miles west of Martinsburgh—giving a route to Baltimore of but 122 miles, which, when the mountain heights avoided are turned into their equivalent in miles, would make the distance virtually no greater than that of the Western Maryland Railroad. This short link of road would be also of incalculable value to the U. S. Government, in facilitating the transportation of troops and supplies from the great valley of Pennsylvania and Maryland into that of Virginia, and thus make its protection of the Baltimore and

Ohio Railroad within the latter state, entirely effective while the war lasts.

By this route Hagarstown would be sixty miles nearer to Baltimore than to Philadelphia, and even Chambersburgh would be fifteen miles the nearest to us. By branching from the Baltimore and Ohio Railroad, at a point nearer to Baltimore, the distance from Hagarstown to our city may be reduced to little over 100 miles, and the difference against Philadelphia increased to some eighty miles, but this would be affected at a considerably increased cost of construction, and would not be required to give us the preference which would be secured by the difference of sixty miles, as far as the current of trade can be influenced by that circumstance.

The citizens of Washington county have begun to awaken to the advantages of a connection with the Baltimore and Ohio Railroad, by the short and level line of moderate cost which is open to them, and overtures have been recently made to that Company with that object which may shortly mature into arrangements for the early construction of a suitable branch road for their accommodation. It is indeed no new idea, for Hagarstown looked thirty years ago, to a connection with this road in the Potomac valley, as the most feasible avenue; properly appreciating the difficulty interposed in the way of a more *apparently* direct route over the lofty mountain forming the eastern boundary of the county of which she is the capital.

The interest of our city in the Baltimore and Ohio Railroad, amounts now, to some $10,000,000, as a stock and bond holder in her corporate capacity. The capital invested in stock and securities of the Company by our citizens, is not much short of $15,000,000, while the state of Maryland, of which our city constitutes one-third of the population and nearly one-half of the property, holds the stock of the Company for near $4,000,000 more. Why then should Baltimore help to build a new road which if it really possesses the advantages claimed for it by its advocates would more or less jeopardize these vast investments? Built, however, as this new road would be, upon a route once deliberately and rightfully rejected as the route of the Baltimore and Ohio Railroad itself, it would be more likely to prove a wasteful outlay of capital in an unprofitable enterprise, than a serious competitor to that road. If Baltimore has any surplus funds to spare, let her rather place them where they will extend and perfect the connections of her great Western line with the railway system of the country, whereby the commercial interests of the city, the state and their citizens, will be promoted and their dividends as shareholders will be increased.

The preceding exposition of this subject has been considered due to this community at this juncture—for surely there is no subject upon which we should be better informed than that of our internal improvements, through which the life blood of our state is brought to its heart—our city. It is much to be regretted that in order to enlighten our citizens on this all important subject, their Chief Magistrate has had to be so often referred to in this connection, but this could not by any means be avoided, for as our people look up to him for correct information upon all matters of public interest, so the consequence of mistakes on his part, are in the highest degree prejudicial to the public welfare. There is no disposition to deal harshly with his errors, as will be seen by the passages in the preceding statements which charge his mistakes upon the bad advisers by whom he has been misled. It is sincerely hoped that hereafter when his Honor speaks or writes about things so seriously affecting the well being of our city, he will be more careful to select disinterested counsellors. We are all liable to be misled by others on whom we must depend more or less for facts which we cannot bring within the sphere of our own personal knowledge, but it behooves those seated in the high places of political office, to exercise the utmost caution in applying to the best sources of information and invoking the best attainable advice in the use of the facts thus obtained. It is feared that his Honor may possibly not receive these friendly hints in the kindly spirit in which they are offered, but the satisfaction arising from the sense of a duty performed to him, as well as to this community, will be not the less experienced by

EXPOSITOR.

www.ingramcontent.com/pod-product-compliance
Lightning Source LLC
LaVergne TN
LVHW010833120826
845149LV00016B/1355

* 9 7 8 1 4 1 8 1 9 0 2 7 9 *